SOULFUEL

A Celebration of Poetry and Song

Clifton Jeffries
www.OurSoulFuel.webs.com
OurSoulFuel@gmail.com

Published by Around H.I.M. Publishing
For publishing information, address:

**Around His Image Marketing and
Publishing**

PO Box 1373
Wake Forest, NC 27588
info@aroundHim.com
www.aroundHim.com

ISBN-10: 098427751X
ISBN-13: 9780984277513

FOREWORD

Giving all glory to GOD for without him there would
be no SOULFUEL..
This book is written with the belief that the reader will
been enlightened, uplifted, and entertained because a
message should not be one dimensional as long as the
positivity is central.
It is the feeling of this author that each page should
touch everyone in some shape, form, or fashion.
SOULFUEL was written with deep passion.
It is a composition of works that covers various
elements of life.
It's FIRE, WATER, WIND and ICE.
SOULFUEL is a sure thing...not a roll of the dice.

ENJOY!
CLIFTON J.

ACKNOWLEDGEMENTS

On bended knees.
Giving thanks to those associated
with Clifton Jeffries.
I wish I could, but if I listed all of your names.
It would be a book in itself.
Thank you. Without you
I could not have done this.
Your feedback. Your pointing out
my miscues.
Keeping me on track.
Help put SOULFUEL in paperback.
So with love, this goes out to all of you.
For business this I must do.
Cover Design: Ricky Garrison
Cover Edit : Ian LaBennett of I Lab Design
1st Edit: Melda Smith
Final Edit: Linda White
Back Cover Photo:Darryl Morrow
Love and Patience: Family
Web Hosting: Ronald McCoy Of McCoy Information
Systems
Document Formulation : Marie Johnson/ Clarence
Holman
My people Will & Sandra Parker Of LULU Publishing.
Adobe Systems
Special thanks...

Ladies and Gentlemen here's the jewel.
Turn the pages and enjoy this SOULFUEL

Table of Contents

Chapter One

PEOPLE
I wrote this book
With the hope
Of reaching people.
Initially, just my people.
I must proclaim
I changed my aim
When I found
We're all the same...
Just people

Soulfuel

SOULFUEL

Descendant of the tribe born to rule
known for dropping verbal jewels.
Spiritually gifted without sitting in pews.
Let me tell you where I get my news...
I walk alongside the man
who leaves footprints in the sand.
Holds my hand, keeps me cool...
Rockin steady on this...

SOULFUEL

Now, bear witness as the gates of knowledge open
allowing this wisdom to flow.
Planting seeds of intelligence
so that intellectually we grow.
Out from this garden wise men will show.
Positively accepting... wanting to reap what they sow.
Understanding how to rule
by being supplied with this...

SOULFUEL

Blessed, cause the Alpha & Omega guides the mind.
Belligerent in their effort to undo this bind
caused by those with blatant disregard for mankind.
Refusing to be left behind, watch we shine.
It's his grace and mercy on which we dine.
So here's your guide, your tool.
These pages separately are spiritual,
but when you combine them...they become

SOULFUEL

I'M ON A MISSION

My mission is to compose these flows
With an intensity that shows.
I stand alongside lyrical pros
That tap the head without physical blows.
Feeding the mind allowing it to grow.
Can I do this? It's for God to bestow.
I get it from him so I'm good to go...
On my mission

I'M ON A MISSION

And with your permission
I'd like to continue to
Hurdle fences using senses
With the intensions of holding court.
See, I'm part of a special sort. I invoke thought.
Deliver a meaning, give it all definition
My vocabulary holds no submission.
Altruism... If you listen you'll hear my mission...

I'M ON A MISSION

And with deep reflection my selection
Is to let love, peace, and harmony be our
Direction. study war no more!
The murders of our babies
Is something we can no longer endure.
God put 'em here. What we killing them for?
Let 'em live, let 'em shine, let 'em glisten
For them to enjoy the fruits of the world
Would be my commission
Just in case you think this is idle talk
Or I'm just whishing, I will be paid in full
I never fail my mission

AND I AM ON A MISSION

LETTER TO THE LORD

To show the pen is mightier than the
Sword.
I took a moment, to write to you
I know you're busy,
And I won't take up much of your
Time.
Just wanted to say... Thank you, for
All, you've done.
I'm so happy... And the reason is,
You chose me to be your sun.
And... What I wanted to know is, can, I,

WALK WITH YOU

On my journey through,
This troubled land.
Can you be there,
To hold my hand?
Can you grant me,
The wisdom to understand,
The knowledge to comprehend,
Your design, your diagram,
So, we have the same plan
What I need to do is,

WALK WITH YOU

BE WITH YOU.

Be like you.
Do what you do.
Not what, man says you do.
So on behalf of myself,
And your, other children too
I send this out... To you.
Cause, love shines thru,

When we

WALK WITH YOU

That's my letter to you.
My lord.

ONE PIECE

One composition, one completion
Regardless of endless nights
Or countless deletions
I wouldn't mind,
And I wouldn't cease
If it took a lifetime to write just...

ONE PIECE

That comes from my heart
And fills your soul.
Has you clapping hands
And tapping your toes.
To God givin flows,
Only heaven knows
How we can feast
If all I composed was just...

ONE PIECE

Maybe a poem, a play
Or just a short story.
a reflection of me
And what I do with harmony.
Verbally reciting,
Spiritually inviting
You to enjoy my writing.
I would be at peace
If all I completed was just...

ONE PIECE

GLORY

To God goes the glory.
To be able to deliver a story
At a time when people are
More interested in Maury.

You are the father.
The truth, the light,
The only time I shine
Is when you direct my mind,
To have my mouth,
Project that sound
That has them... Gathered round.
Standing still, and still getting down
Only God can get this...

GLORY

That ability to mediate.
To show a strength.
That can no longer wait.
To give love.
The victory over hate.
To appreciate
The spiritual mandate
That flows from heaven's gate.
I can't wait. It's a true story....

IT'S GOD'S GLORY

YOU GOD

I love the way this thing is flowing.
I love the way this thing is going.
We're in control, thankful for knowing
The reason we continue growing is....

YOU GOD

This is your earth. You gave it birth.
Taught me its value, it's worth.
When you created the heavens,
The night the day, you also supplied
Me with the ability to pray, to say, to stay with...

YOU GOD

And I choose right over wrong.
I choose to create not just get along.
I choose to write verses,
That make my people strong.
And if you're my people,
It doesn't matter what color you have on.
It's easy. Not hard you riding with me?
Then you're riding with g.o.d.
Take a knee. Nod.
We give all praises to the almighty...

YOU GOD

SPIRITUAL MANDATE

Before we can pass thru heaven's gate,
We need to demonstrate
That we can regulate
And appreciate a spiritual mandate.
First, we must get our house in order.
Make a woman out of our daughter.
A man from our son.
Then don't just settle for a crumb.
Be properly compensated.
Stop living in a mental slum.
Get your worth. Don't hesitate...

THAT'S A SPIRITUAL MANDATE

Don't accept misery
As part of your destiny.
Truly work hard
To achieve prosperity.
Reaching deep down within your anatomy
To bring out something I would love to see.
That Soulfuel prophecy.
When we apply understanding to
Humanity...
And I can't wait...

FOR THAT SPIRITUAL MANDATE

In the words of
Martin, Malcolm and Marvin,
I know you're starvin
Like me for that reality.
See, I too have a dream,
And by any means necessary
Let's get it on.
Let this be the new negro spiritual.
Speaking words of wisdom,

Let it be, let it be, a spiritual reality.
Sign it into law. Something they never seen
Before.
And don't you dare hate. It's ordained...

IT'S A SPIRITUAL MANDATE

MAYA ANGELOU
Respect to you
I wrote before I read you.
Now, when I read you,
Emulate you, I hope to

MS. ANGELOU

Because of you, I rise.
Transcribe from deeper inside.
When my words provide
An Angelou definition
I've arrived.

Not just writing,
Reciting, igniting.
Doing my thing.
I know why the caged bird sings.
Blessed to have my voice.
Talk about love,
And the peace it brings
Because of you...

MAYA ANGELOU.

GOOD BYE TO A FRIEND

The beginning. Not the end.
On earth a family eternal kin.
I know you went to heaven,
So I know we'll meet again.

That's why my heart smiles
When I recall a life line worthwhile.
I remember my grandmother
In her strongest of days.
Home cooked meals, fresh biscuits,
Filled the trays and no one eats
Until everyone prays.

Her existence was spent on Gods throne.
His religion was her backbone.
Seems as thou she was here on loan,
To reach and teach. And from her I learned
It matters not what anyone thinks.
Trust me. Cause I wondered
How she could spend so much
Time at that kitchen sink.

For you see, she had done her thing a longtime
Ago.
It was God she was waiting for. At that kitchen
Window.
Some question... Where has he been.
Was he like her blown... Away with the wind?
Well, while you conspired
To divvy up trinkets and petty cash
My grandmother was spiritually
Giving me her soul to put in my stash.
I unknowingly mourned in a different way.
I never saw weak so I have nothing weak to say.
I'll carry a picture of strength to my dying
Day.

That's where I've been. So it's so long...

NEVER GOODBYE MY FRIEND

SETTLED NOW

Back from the dead
To write what you've read.
Survived a battle with drugs.
Those battles with thugs.
Lost loves.
Nights I thought
I was headed for the heavens above
To pitch poetic nouns. I must be..

SETTLED NOW

Thankful to be around.
Shed that gangster now.
No more underground.
Foundation is what it's about now.
To God goes the glory.
That's my royal crown.
Know what?... I'm...

SETTLED NOW

Tell you what I found.
A subtle sound
Used properly
Pound for pound
Can endow a town.
Quicker than any hate
Can tear it down.
24/7 profound
Is how I'm coming at you now.
Settle down. I'm just...

SETTLED NOW

Chapter Two

ONE
In order for one to teach
One must be learned.
In order for one to reach,
One must teach what one has learned

ONE

BRING IT ON

Whatever you got for me..
No matter what it is..
It don't matter what it is..

BRING IT ON

I stand tall so you can see,
This light I got around me.
It's the lord God almighty.
And he's shining on my left and right.
I walk this path to stay in sight.
I pray to him every night. So...

BRING IT ON

Whatever you got for me..
No matter what it is..
It don't matter what it is...

BRING IT ON

I got a force that's very real.
It's a force you're gonna feel
If you disturb God and his will.
His plan is for me to rise
With him walking by my side. And, if
If you think you can break my stride
Your wrong...

BRING IT ON.

JESUS WORKS

Sometimes in your life,
You reach a certain point.
Hopefully you'll discover, yeah.

That it's time to make a change.
That it's time to take control.
That it's time to take command.

TIME TO TAKE JESUS, JESUS BY THE HAND.
OH, YEAH

Cause it's your life, that you're living.
He will help you understand,
What it is you're going thru.

Talk to him, let him tell you,
Let him tell you what to do.
And I'm sure he will, tell you,

That it's time to make a change.
That it's time to take control.
That it's time to take command.

TIME TO TAKE JESUS, TAKE JESUS BY THE
HAND

JESUS WORKS

THANK YOU
I WANT TO SAY
THANK YOU, THANK YOU, THANK YOU.

Whether you know or not,
You have a special friend.
Someone you can count on,
To be there 'til the end.
In your time of troubles,
On him you can depend.

Who is that special one? (Jesus)
He's your special friend.

I WANT TO SAY
(THANK YOU, THANK YOU, THANK YOU.)

When your mind is weary.
And your heart is low.
You're so very lucky,
You have a place to go.
Where you can lift your head.
Let your spirit grow.
Where's that special place? (heaven)
The house of your special friend

I WANT TO SAY
(THANK YOU, THANK YOU, THANK YOU.)

For being there for me.
When I felt so all alone.
I didn't have anyone
I could call on the phone.
I got down on my knees,
I said lord, would you please
Let me have the keys...
To that special place (heaven)

Where I can speak
To my special friend (Jesus)

I WANT TO SAY
(THANK YOU, THANK YOU, THANK YOU)

I ADORE YOU
DID YOU KNOW THAT I ADORE YOU

I watch the sun rise. I watch it fall.
Yes, these times are captivating
But the best time of the day it seems
Is when you're standing next to me.

DID YOU KNOW THAT I ADORE YOU
I ADORE YOU

I wish that I could hold your hand.
But the thought of you is all I have.
I think about you constantly
Wanting you here with me.

DID YOU KNOW THAT I ADORE YOU
I ADORE YOU

My days, my nights ,they run together.
I have no concept of time or weather
When you're with me.
Things are much better.
So come to me. Oh! Come to me.
Be with me. Please stay with me...

DID YOU KNOW THAT I ADORE YOU
I ADORE YOU

GOD SPEAKS TO ME

God speaks to me.
And I'm telling you
That God will love you
If you love yourself.

Now, that's the message.
That he gave to me.
So, I'm telling you
God will love you
If you love yourself.

God speaks to me.
And I'm telling you
God will love you
If you love yourself.

He said it's easy.
Not very hard to do.
Hear the words I say.
For every one is true.
God will love you
If you love yourself.

God speaks to me.
And I'm telling you,
That God will love you
If you love yourself.

Everybody, everybody,
Everybody, everybody.
God will love you,
If you love yourself.

GOD SPEAKS TO ME

HEAVENLY FATHER

HEAVENLY FATHER
HOLY REDEEMER

Can you hold my hand?
I need you to guide me
Thru this troubled land.
I've tried on my own but
To no avail.
With you beside me,
I know I cannot fail.

HEAVENLY FATHER
HOLY REDEEMER

I'm reaching out to you.
For your grace and mercy.
There's nothing I won't do.
Climb the highest mountain,
Swim the deepest sea.
If it brings you closer,
Closer, closer to me.

HEAVENLY FATHER
HOLY REDEEMER

I stand before your eyes.
I'm your creation.
So I know you're not surprised.
I want to be with you.
And loves the reason why.
I give my all to you.
My heart and soul to you...

HEAVENLY FATHER
HOLY REDEEMER

IT COMES FROM GOD
IT COMES FROM GOD

It all comes from God
The life we live
Gifts to give
Breath we breathe
The birds and bees
Come from God

It all comes from God
Woman and man
A ground to stand
Songs we sing
Love and harmony
Comes from God

It all comes from God
The light that shines
Is yours and mine
The night and days
The prayer we pray
Comes from God

IT ALL COMES FROM GOD

UNDESCRIBABLE

Since the first time I met you,
I never could forget you.
You turned my world around.
Showed me how to stand my ground.
And what I'd like to say is,
That you mean so much to me.
And let me portray that
It was you that set me free.
The way I feel about you is so...

UNDESCRIBABLE

My light... My shining star.
I can feel you no matter where you are.
Everything is you
In the world I find wonderful.
You make my everyday
In the world seem so beautiful.
Words cannot describe
What's going on inside my mind.
And what I like to say is you're so...

UNDESCRIBABLE

You said I can live free.
Then granted me the victory.
Turned my gray sky's blue,
Making all my dreams come true.
Now I'm yearning for your love.
Wanting you to hold me in your arms
With a feeling from the heavens above.
Flying higher than I've flown before.
It's unbelievable... My life's unbelievable...
You're so

UNDESCRIBABLE

I'M ON MY WAY

Oh lord, won't you show me the direction
In which to travel
To get to your house.

Oh lord, if tomorrow
I had to come home
Please prepare me
For the journey.

Oh lord, the road is lonely
To where I'm going
And you're the only
One walking with me.

I'M ON MY WAY

Oh lord, I can feel your
Soothing spirit
Deep down inside me

As you guide me.
Oh lord, I want to thank you
For that feeling...
That heavenly feeling...
That you give me.

I'M ON MY WAY

GO TO GOD

Go to God when you're down and lonely.
Go to God cause he's the only...
The only one that makes it better...
The lord makes it better...
Ask the lord to make it better...
And he'll make it better for you.

Nothing in your life is going right.
You feel like you want to give up.
That's the time you need to stand up.
Give the lord... The lord some worship.

Go to God when you're down and lonely.
Go to God cause he's the only...
The only one that makes it better...
The lord makes it better...
Ask the lord to make it better...
And he'll make it better for you.

Trying to solve all of your problems.
Trying with all of your might.
God always said it's his battle.
So go ahead and put in his hands.

The hole you dig gets deeper and deeper.
The hill you climb gets steeper and steeper.
The love you lost is nowhere to be found.
Don't give up. He's always around.

Go to God when you're down and lonely.
Go to God cause he's the only...
The only one that makes it better...
Ask the lord to make it better...
And he'll make it better for you.

GO TO GOD

Chapter Three

GEM

Here's a gem.
Just a whim
My shoes
Are jewels
You can't
Comprehend
Until you've
Walked a mile
In them.

GEM

UNIQUE BEAT

Thank you for this opportunity to speak.
For you know now, that when I speak
I speak straight to my people.
So bold, so black, so beautiful.
I love you... That's why I chill
As I spill in this bo-willied style.
With a glow... Heaven knows flows. Straight
From the Nile.
See this is about us and what we do
And why whatever we do, we make look easy.
We're prim... We're prop...
Ain't nothing about us sleazy.
And now that you understand
How I'm flowing,
Sit back, relax, and I'll keep going.
As I continue to recite from this menu
About that beat... Formentioned. Yo... It's in you.
That base, that scratch, that natural attack.
Flowing straight thru your veins from way,
Way, back.
That dazzling intellect that you can't help
But to project.
Manifesting itself so greatly, if I didn't possess
It myself, I too
Would be upset. And oh... Not to mention the
Way you move.
So sweet. So silky. So smooth.
A combination like this
Makes me wonder how you ever lose.
I'll tell you how that's done.
By flipping the script...
Changing the message.
Sending one extremely alarming.
You continue to kill your brethren.
You're just killing your army.
Your strength comes in numbers

That's a mathematical fact.
Straight up... On that subject we're stupid.
I think you already know that.
So from now on when you listen
Don't just listen search inside your soul
And pay attention to your own

UNIQUE BEAT

A beat that directs you. That corrects you
As a matter of fact, it's a direct reflection of
You.
When you close two eye's and open the third,
Believe what you see inside. Never mind what
You've heard.
Feel that rhythm that flows thru your body.
It's the reason you move like you move.
Although you ain't at a party. It's given to you.
'Cause you're special son.
Stand up... Be proud... You are the chosen one.
You've been granted victory... over defeat.my
People... You possess your own...

UNIQUE BEAT

ENGLISH

With the brush of a pen I send a message to
Them.
Them that comprehend
That we are of them
That stroked and swam. Descendants of trips
Aboard deadly ships.
Shackled in chains. Unclothed when it rained.
Still maintain. Chose not to sleep
With the fish.
Arrived at your shores and learned your...

ENGLISH

Quickly coming to grips.
With my new authority and our relationship.
Yes, I hope this rips
Into your moral fiber.
Deep down into your loins,
Your dollars to my coins.
I can only bet what I get.
Fought the same wars
But don't receive the same benefits.
These are facts, not comments
That I put into...

ENGLISH

We're close, but by far unless
We can touch it, it's no cigar.
It's bazar and I try
To figure the reason why.
On TV I still see my people cry.
Pardon me, I don't mean to pry.
But are you not looking out
Your left and right eye.
Do you not see...

The despair, the misery?
Is it just me
Or is it complacency?
Where's your decency?
You have to fight if you wish
To continue to speak...

ENGLISH

SOLDIERS

Look how we stand.
So royal, so regal, so grand.
'Though spawned on a different continent
There's no fear of standing here.
Tall, strong, poised. Ready to take command.

Not getting it twisted. Not trying to own all
This land.
Except for thee on which we stand.
Once we touched it, it was ours,
That was granted by divine powers.

My people continue to check it.
As I share with you
These rhythm less rhymes,
You might want to parlay
These gems from my mind.
Thoughts about diversity,
Prosperity, determination, collaboration...
The coming together of a nation.
The rebuilding of our blocks.
The investing in ourselves.
Then flipping bonds and stocks.

Now, as for me I live this sh _ _.
I don't just perform.
I'm constantly getting it on.
If you want to ride with me
Thru the storm, Son I'll be easy to see.
I'll be the one on the horse
At the break of dawn.

Come join me and together.
We can ride... Off into the sunset...

LIKE SOLDIERS

PICTURE LIVING RIGHT

Reflections from the lake
Upon which I gaze.
Falling leaves,
Causing light waves.
Ripples in the water
Lit by moon rays.
Couldn't have
These cool nights
Without good days.
Those perfect segues
To reaching higher heights...

I PICTURE LIVING RIGHT

Being one with the breeze
That flows thru the trees.
Rooted, grounded.
Humbly down on my knees.
Thanking you for giving me
The opportunity
To share a world with elements
That span the centuries...

I PICTURE LIVING RIGHT

With images of elevation
Being the revelation
That comes to pass.
Us caring for one another
Is the only way. We're going to last.
Keeping victory in sight.
Oh, say can you see
Us close nit and tight.
The perfect picture....

OF LIVING RIGHT

I REMINISCE

I live kool and relaxed.
I grew up vibin' to the sounds of
Miles and his sax.
Reminiscing about the days
Those beats came on wax.
I know, 'cause I recorded them on
Cassettes and 8 tracks.

I remember the nights.
Street lights .
Parties in the park.
Freakin in the dark.
Our cable for all intent
Was funkadelic. Parliament.

I REMINISCE

Back in the day
Blackberry was a brandy.
We paid a penny for candy.
Held on to our brothers ,
Cause they came in handy.
Walked with pride, even if our
Clothes were a little randy.

Only mind freak I could find
Was the way she shook her behind.
My reality TV. Good times.
Flavor Flav recited rhymes
With chuck-d content militarized.
Back when the mob didn't drop dimes.
A famous James Brown line... Pick up on this...

AS I REMINISCE

BLACKMAN

I stick. I slam

Build bricks

Blend hands

I be him...

Blackman.

Long heart

Short fear

Tap baby

And I be there

Walk hard

Look small

Run, ride

Hide, crawl...

Blackman.

And at twilight

Stand tall.

Stretched, burned

Black hands

Shinny metallic

Unyielding

I be him...

Blackman.

HISTORY

History is how you should start your biography.
Your direction in which to write your trilogy.
By paying homage to those truly holy.
Those that proceeded thee like
Booker T, firebrick. D, the Buffalo Soldiers.
That's how you came to be.
It's scripture. A perfect group of three.
Your origination began...

HISTORY

That railroad to freedom.
Pullman, pioneered by Harriet Tubman
And a host of other sisters and brothers.
Comprised of all colors with the same goal
To break the chain of hatred
That's had our nation in a strong hold.
My country tears of thee
Sweet land of liberty
That is your

HISTORY

Oh say, do you see?
Our duty is preservation
Not the destruction of humanity.
Not the best bombs, not the best arms,
Unlocked doors, not the best alarms.
Having the best farms, growing the best food,
Not using crude... Oil, if it spoils our ecology.
How bout the g.n.p? Not guns and drugs as a legacy.
I don't ask for much,
But if you would do this for me?
"cause before I die, I'd like to write a positive....

HISTORY

THE PAST

Since the past is the past,
On that for a moment let us dwell.
Let's compile all the facts
And see what stories they tell.
Let's take his-story, lay it out like a map.
Now we can see exactly why
We are where we're at.

Then, let's acknowledge
That most of his-story is a lie.
It's geared to give some
A false since of bravado
And others, no hope at all for tomorrow.

And before you get to thinking
That this is the same old same,
Quite the contrary.
It's a formula, on how to play the game.
The truth will now form your foundation.
Your foundation based on true information
Will supply the fuel that feeds your
Determination.
To alleviate any negative situation.
And the truth is you're standing on it.
It's been beneath you all the time.
Now make up your own mind.
All your life you've been told
To keep your head up.
Keep your head up.
Only problem with that is
If you never look down
How are you going to tell
If you're stepping onto solid ground? You need
You need to look where you step
To see where you're going.
Have your facts together

So that when you get there
You're amongst the knowing.
Be clever in your every endeavor.
Research it, be prepared for whatever.
Check out his-story. Make sure
It matches what's in your heart.
'Cause the truth is in you. God wrote that part.
Now I didn't say this first, but I will say it last.
Create your own positive his-story
And you won't
Have a repeat of the...

PAST

FROM MY HEART

Normally, I'd go buy a card
Filled with the words
I find hard to express.
Today, I'll take a shot.
I'll do my best.
See, it's you
I want to impress
With the words you read...

COMING FROM MY HEART

Simply implying, I love you
And never want to part
From you and your loving ways.
It resembles the calming effects
We experience from
The sounds of the rain.
Life's been better
Since the day you came.
This I profess and proclaim.
With you in my arms
Is how I want to remain
Forever...

AND THAT'S FROM MY HEART

MASSAGE

It starts with a warm tub of water,
A little wine some cheese.
Her favorite book.
Making sure everything is in order.
Turn off the phone. Dim the lights.
The temperature of the oil is just
Right.
Sheets. A thick terry... On the night
Stand.
Hot chocolate and strawberries.
All this is necessary for your...

MASSAGE

If you like I'll sit and talk with you
While you lie in the tub.
So when you need your back done I'm
There to rub place's you can't reach.
The soaps a creamy peach.
No dream, no illusion, no mirage.
Are you ready for your ...

MASSAGE

Good. Step out get toweled down.
Rap this clothe around
Your beautiful frame.
And this second towel here is for
Your hair.
When you're, done come on in here
And get your...

MASSAGE

Lay upon pedals made of rose.
Let the hot oil penetrate your toes

And the rest of your feet.
Take a bite of this berry
Dipped in chocolate so sweet.
Then, a sip of wine
As I do your calves, knees , and
Thighs.
Slowing down at the base of your
Spine.
'Cause from here I go straight to
Your mind.
Oh yeah... I left a dozen rose's out in
The garage.
Did you want them before or after
Your...

MASSAGE...?

Chapter Four

HEY KING
It doesn't take a
Wise man to see
It's not your home
When the contents
Of the castle
Does not include
Your throne.

HEY KING

A WOMAN

You know a woman needs a man,
that makes her feel like she has a man.
One thing you must try and do,
is everything that your woman wants you to.
If she has, a problem be there by her side.
If she needs direction, you must be her guide.
Be more than a lover. You must be friend.
Let her know you'll be there to the very end.

YOU KNOW A WOMAN NEEDS A MAN.
THAT MAKE HER FEEL LIKE SHE HAS A MAN.

Look your baby in her eyes,
put your right hand on her thighs.
With your left hand, pull her close.
Gently kiss her cheek.
Tell her she can get this kind of lovin'
seven days a week.

Like roses on the table when she gets home.
Hot oil & a back rub with a glass of wine.
Soothing conversation to relax her mind.
Mellow music in the background.
Set this sexy scene
Now you can lay her down.
Kiss her from her head down to her toes,
and if she has them on, rip off those pantyhose.

YOU KNOW A WOMAN NEEDS A MAN.
THAT MAKES HER FEEL LIKE SHE HAS A MAN.

HERE WITH ME

HERE WITH ME
HERE WITH ME

Where you're
Supposed to be.
Living life
Day and night
Is only right
When you're here with me.

HERE WITH ME
HERE WITH ME

Feeling free.
Flying high.
Reason why
Is you're here with me.

HERE WITH ME
HERE WITH ME

It's harmony.
Please believe
My destiny
Is clear when you're...

HERE WITH ME
HERE WITH ME

THICK
I LIKE E'M THICK & RICH-OOH & CHOCOLATE

Those thighs, those eyes.
Girl I'm mesmerized
By those lips, those hips.
You know I've got a plan
Take me by the hand.
Come and go with me to ecstasy.
Baby don't you know
Girl how you make me grow..
.

CAUSE YOU'RE THICK & RICH-OOH & CHOCOLATE

Hot pants. Tight shirt.
Makes me wanna work
On that back, that neck.
Girl, I'm just a wreck
When you move you shake.
Hope it's real not fake.
Girl for goodness sake.

YOU'RE SO THICK & RICH-OOH & CHOCOLATE

On the street I savor
Chocolate in every flavor.
Some short, some tall
When they walk down the hall
I want to taste them all.
And I love being in the sheets
With the girl with the healthy cheeks...

THAT'S SO THICK & RICH-OOH & CHOCOLATE

WICKED WITCH

When we lie in bed at night
You know just what I wish.
'Cause when I think of you
My mind becomes so rich.
Filled with the thoughts of love
My body starts to twitch.

You make me so hot girl
I rip off every stitch

SEE YOU'RE MY WICKED WICKED WITCH.
HEY YEAH, MY WICKED WICKED WITCH
BABY SCRATCH MY ITCH

Then you whisper in my ear.
You see it's time to play.
You say just lay back baby
And let me do my way.
Now it's not the things you say,
But definitely the things you do.
You're so naughty girl.
You make me wicked too.

CAUSE YOU'RE MY WICKED WICKED WITCH
HEY YEAH, MY WICKED WICKED WITCH
BABY SCRATCH MY ITCH.

Now wait a minute girls.
Please let me explain.
It's the things that she does
It drives me insane.
That's the reason
I use the name. (pause)
Wicked baby, hey yeah

TIME IS WASTING

The moment I saw your lovely face
I knew right then how good you would
Taste.
Pretty brown complexion and long dark
Hair
Made me stop, stand, still and stare.

Chocolate covered, candy sweet.
She's the girl I've been dying to meet.
A definite dime that's built real fine.
Gotta find a way to make that girl mine.

Time is wasting. Time to get down.
Time to get busy.
Got to get her somehow.

Say hey pretty baby. Come on over here.
Let me whisper a little something in your
Ear.
You came, with your girls.
How bout you leave out
With a bonafide man that'll make you
Scream and shout.

Come back and get this lovin like
Every day.
You look so good it makes me wanna say
That I'm not gonna waste another beat of
The clock. Gonna hit that body steady and make it
Rock

Time is wasting. Time to get down.
Time to get busy.
Got to get her somehow...

TIME IS WASTING

UMM

EVERY SECOND "UMM,"
EVERY MINUTE "UMM,"
OF EVERY HOUR "UMM..."

Baby this is real. It's about how you Feel.
As I whisper in your ear just how
Much I care,
Squeeze your body tight. Ready to go All night.

EVERY SECOND "UMM,"
OF EVERY MINUTE "UMM,"
OF EVERY HOUR "UMM."

All see is you and the things you do.
Kissing on your lips, then your finger Tips.
Gently around your eye's down to
Your thighs.

EVERY SECOND "UMM,"
OF EVERY MINUTE "UMM,"
OFEVERY HOUR "UMM."

As I stroke you there, gently pull Your hair
I'll touch your every spot. The one's
That make you hot
No I'm not done yet , just getting
Started. Making you sweat

EVERY SECOND "UMM,"
OF EVERY MINUTE "UMM,"
OF EVERY HOUR "UMM,"

I DO IT EASY

I keep it verbal smooth
Now, peep an achiever in this millennium.
One blessed with the gift to create plennium.
One who sits and sense without a drum.
By writing with the best of them.
It's God's gift. That's how come
My voice supplies the rhythm
As I deliver the rhymes.
Vocally soothing to the mind.
Flowing this way each and every time...

I DO IT EASY

I keep it verbal smooth
I dip as I rip these verses'
With a force you'll
Fill down in your hips
As though I had sailed
Aboard those deadly ships
But I ain't mad
This ain't no chip
Just here to ensure those that follow
Have a clue got a grip
So enjoy the trip

AS I DO IT EASY

And keep it verbal smooth
Don't do much dancing...
Only the octaves move.
Elevating, stimulating
My peoples groove.
Taster's choice.
I'm the one they choose for givin understanding
With a message so commanding.

There's no way they can lose.
See the answers in your soul.
So let your soul take control.
I'll supply the fuel you grab a hold.
The ride i provide
Makes you feel strong inside.
It's been tough that can't be denied.
Heaven knows I'm just doing shows
I'm taking my blues and flipping
Them into jewels
That hopefully one day will be thought in schools. As
Long as I follow my on rules
And that's

TO DO IT EASY
AND KEEP IT VERBAL SMOOTH

KOOL BOP

KOOL BOP... KOOL BOP.
Check it. Smooth base thumpin'. Big wheels Spinnin'.
Steppin' out in the finest of linen.
Before I got here the baddest of women
Is where I was swimmin'.
When I leave, it'll be the same
That's why I'm grinnin'.
Come test if u must. I'm winnin'.
You knew this from the beginnin'.
Or if you didn't, do your homework
As I drive the ladies berserk with this

KOOL BOP KOOL BOP

That's how we rock.
Flossed to the core. Keepin' it cooler
Then it's ever been before.
Yet, so hot. It's my ice that stops
Me from meltin' this spot.
When I hit the block, I'm too deep.
Don't let those things pop.
Don't get buried with the crop.
You're better off with that

KOOL BOP KOOL BOP

Brim sported, ace duce.
Nice off that thing I got from Bruce.
Coupled with that goose.
Keeps me feelin loose.
No war tonight. U' might wanna
Call a truce and throw your hands
In the air. Raise the roof. Tell the truth.

The hottest is this...

KOOL BOP KOOL BOP

JUST WANTED TO SAY
Started out so innocent.
Falling so deeply in love
Not my intent.
Never had a clue.
No idea it would be you.
Not mad actually quite glad.
Could not have asked for a
Better mate
Never had a longer date

JUST WANTED TO SAY

The nights are long
When you are gone
Constantly calling on the phone.
Sitting alone in this empty chair
Whole while wishing you were here
May sound like I got it bad
Like I should be mad, on the
Contrary quite glad
Could not have asked for a
Better mate
Never had a longer date

JUST WANTED TO SAY

Every day is like brand new
Finding it hard to believe
Found someone true
Had no idea it would be you
Mad, on the other hand. Real glad

Could not have asked for a
Better mate
Never had a longer date

JUST WANTED TO SAY

I SING OUT LOUD
If you're like me
Sometimes you feel a little down
Let me tell about
This joy I found
I point my head
Straight to the clouds
I lift my voice with a holy sound

I SING OUT LOUD

From deep inside
To let you know
What's on my mind
I've got this feeling
Down in my soul
It kinda sorta
Makes me lose control

AND I SING OUT LOUD

With all my might
To bring you pleasure
Make you feel alright
I'll keep it mellow
I'll keep it smooth
I'll raise my voice and
Make your spirit move

I'LL SING OUT LOUD

Chapter Five

EXPERIENCE
The only way to prove
You've been any place
Is to describe where
You've been.
The only way to prove
You've done anything
Is to finish what you
Began.

EXPERIENCE

LADIES RISE

Ladies rise... Claim life as your prize.
Show the world that you've arrived.
Give them the wisdom... The mind
So they'll see how you provide.
Sweet music in the air.
A little piece of tender lovin' care.
An inner beauty that enhances
Gods entire atmosphere.

LADIES RISE.

Come take a ride. On this journey our mission
Will be To right the wrongs of humanity.
Halt the killings and atrocities.
Who's better suited than she?
The one who gives us life from her body.
Ultimately, to achieve any victory
You must do, not just try... Now...

LADIES RISE.

And this is how you stride,
With your heads held high.
Determination in your eyes.
A strength that can't be denied.
Maintained by the endurance you supply.
A will... Only rivaled by the most high.
You must realize that you have to rise
In order for the world to survive.

LADIES RISE

Is that not what you do when you hear your
Babies cry?

LADIES RISE

EIGHT JOINTS

Eight joints to completion
And this pie is done.
Cut into fifty piece's
So the whole world
Can get some in...

EIGHT JOINTS

Come get your fill.
Probably won't reach the table
So be prepared
To catch as I spill
Gods will in...

EIGHT JOINTS

To bring to a close
The first of a saga
With an understanding
That this comes from a father
Who stands alongside his father.
And if I didn't love you
I wouldn't bother
To talk about
What I talk about with my father.
I'll release all these points in...

EIGHT JOINTS

BAKE

Mix. Mix. Shake. Shake...

TASTE.

When the flavor's right...

BAKE.

Don't reach for that oven
Til' you add that lovin' ingredient.
That content that'll get 'em bent
Pleasing to the fullest extent is when you...

BAKE.

You'll know when it's ready.
And until it's ready,
You mix, mix, shake, shake...

TASTE

That's how you...

BAKE

ON THIS NIGHT
Oh.... What a night.
Such a delight.
Everything is just right.
Skies filled with stars of light.
The moon is shining bright.
Words of insight keeps me tight.
Not to share this moment
Would be impolite...

ON THIS NIGHT

I write... To define
The syllables I combine.
The reason that they rhyme
Is so that my people continue to climb
And stay on one accord.
After all, we've endured.
It's time we soared
In the twilight. It's for peace I reach...

ON THIS NIGHT

Not thoughts of columbine,
Nor deaths in Iraq, or Africa
Can cloud my mind.
Nights like this are one of a kind.
So I come before you
With a benediction
Filled with true conviction.
Cause I adore you.
Life to me is special... Very.to my inner circle
I flow like a broken levee.
But, it's seldom The world hears me recite
And I chose to do it...

ON THIS NIGHT

AFRICA

Ever heard of her... The mother land
And her horrible existence?
For instance, we stripped her of her
Natural resources to include her people.
Set courses to lands to be their bosses.
Strapped on harnesses like they were horses.
Tore up families. Hold no remorse's.

AFRICA

Found a cure for cancer. Went back to her.
Infected her with aids in order to continue to get paid.
Manufactured your pharmaceuticals
Insured by them that found slavery profitable.
New York Life, Penn Mutual,
And if I didn't mention you that
Does not make you less responsible,
For the plight of...

AFRICA

If you think I'm passing blame, don't bother.
Because a lot of blame goes to its fathers.
Their selfishness and greed. A major factor indeed.
With that being said, let's take this opportunity and
Give the motherland what she needs.
That's to heal the babies that bleed,
Administer the vaccines to cure their disease.
Hydrate the land where God first grew trees.
Close the door on civil war.
Stop the killing of millions. Bring peace to a region
That in our lifetime we've never seen before.
Not for me. Not for you. But for her.
It's your mothers land...

AFRICA

COME TAKE A RIDE

Come on. Take a ride. Buckle up.
We're bout to go deep inside.
The wisdom we'll provide.
Allows you to realize.
We don't demote or chastise.
That won't help the world to rise
Or our seeds to grow.
That we planted and nurtured
To be the leaders of tomorrow.

WE WANT TO RIDE

Not in the ground, but while on top
As the champagne bottles pop.
We want to toast, we want to host
Our life like yours to us means the most.

COME TAKE THIS RIDE

While the road is clear ,
Drive on over here.
What awaits you
Is the opportunity,
To beautify the atmosphere.
Every one you touch, and every one you see
So that my country I no longer shed tears for thee.
If you're gonna be the example of liberty
You need to start with your own community.
The world is watching...

COME TAKE A RIDE

NO TITLE

To this there is no title
This is a spiritual recital
Nothing particular in mind
Just the progressive way I spend my time
How I talk out loud before I even open my mouth
By typing in the positives
Then speaking without doubt
No questions, no answers, no solutions.
To life's game
Loving life is my claim to fame
So for me life will remain the same
Steady as I grow
Not affected by the high or low
I'm Gods son in case you didn't know

NO TITLE

No subject, no object-tion
I understand the process
Of how this thing is done
I'm feeding off of what's being fed
Staying heavenly to the core body and head
And you may be well versed and well read
But you've read nothing
Till you read what God said
See me I'm solid stone I span several ages
Like having fun but don't get too outrageous
I just hope you love what I put on these pages
And I hope this positivity is contagious
Yes I've been around for a minute
Bout to get up in it
I'm taking what God puts in my head and pen it
Then package it up and send it...
Out to let you know
What me and our farther talk about
I worship what's in my heart not an idol

This Soulfuel has me feeling so good inside
I call it my bible
But there's one thing I forgot to do
And that's give this piece a title
So to this...

THERE IS NO TITLE

I KNOW NOT

I know not who I am,
Nor who I truly be.
The name I use is not
The one God gave to me.
Yet, through it all
He chose to let me be.
To let me find. To let me
Search. Is this land my
Place of birth
Or did I originate
Somewhere else on this earth?

I KNOW NOT

As I look in the mirror,
The fact that I am
Not what I'm called
Becomes much clearer.
Though my history
Is clouded in mystery,
I'm not giving in that easily.
I stand tall for the world
To see what a man looks
Like thru adversity.
How do I keep going?
Why is it that when I move
It's like my fingers pop

I KNOW NOT

I just keep humming
I just keep coming
Deep down in my soul
The funky drummers drumming
I be he. The one so stunning
Track star.

But only for the truth
Will you see me running
Standing my ground
Being profound
Is how it's going down
Don't care if you like me now
No more slave mentality
Is it biblical for me
To have just reach this reality

I KNOW NOT.

BUT I DO KNOW...
I WON'T STOP.

NOW

Not now but right now
As the past, present and future coincide.
Before one is done, the other provides.
Us with a stimulus to continue to stride
The past being the bank.
The present making deposits
So that the future can collect the dividends.
This is the one where everybody wins.
This is the one about... Fun in the sun.
This is the one about... Here you go.
I told you. I got you. We've only just begun
Laying in the shade. Mimosa's hand made.
Kids draped. Everybody's paid.
The bank... That mental deposit.
Dividends justified cause we never quit
Paying attention is how we profit
Here let me draw you a composite
A picture and you're the only one in it
Yours is the only money that is tracked
I goggled it . It's a fact
So this is what we do about that
We take the 500.billion to the 1.1 trillion spent annually
Spend it in our community
And make our children the beneficiary

NOT YESTERDAY...
NOT TOMORROW...
NOT NOW...

BUT
RIGHT... NOW

DREAM

Reach for that unreachable star.
Be who you are.
In life this will take you very far
Blend your present with your past
So that you hit the future in stride on full blast.
Be informed. The exception... Not the norm.
The opportunity to be informed
Is a blessing that elevates you
From a shower to a storm.

GO AHEAD AND DREAM

You go ahead and believe
And if tomorrow is granted
For you know it's not promised.
You go with God speed.
He built you for battle.
He will not leave you without
giving you what you need.
Your commander and chief.
Only He can fill a life with joy desecrated by grief.

DREAM

Be a beam be pristine go ahead and scream
And whether or not anyone else deems... It improbable
God makes all things possible.
Take it from one who knows.
It took a life -time to deliver these flows.
And if I hadn't gone thru what I went thru
I couldn't convince you to believe in your...

DREAM

CHURCH

www.ingramcontent.com/pod-product-compliance
Lightning Source LLC
LaVergne TN
LVHW051709080426
835511LV00017B/2811